Been There,
Survived That

First published in 2008 by
Zest Books, an imprint of Orange Avenue Publishing
35 Stillman Street, Suite 121, San Francisco, CA 94107
www.zestbooks.net

Created and produced by Zest Books, San Francisco, CA
© 2008 by Orange Avenue Publishing LLC
Illustrations © 2008 by Dick Hill

Text set in Cushing; title text set in Memphis

Teen Nonfiction / High School

Library of Congress Control Number: 2007939160
ISBN-13: 978-0-9790173-7-7
ISBN-10: 0-9790173-7-8

CREDITS
EDITORIAL DIRECTOR: Karen Macklin
CREATIVE DIRECTOR: Hallie Warshaw
WRITERS/TEEN ADVISORY BOARD: Carolyn Hou, Maxfield J. Peterson,
                             Joe Pinsker, Hannah Shr
EDITOR: Karen Macklin
ILLUSTRATOR: Dick Hill
COVER AND INTERIOR DESIGN: Cari McLaughlin
PRODUCTION ARTIST: Cari McLaughlin

Printed in China.
First printing, 2008
10 9 8 7 6 5 4 3 2 1

Been There, Survived That

Getting Through Freshman Year of High School

Edited by Karen Macklin

I t's the first day of school. You're walking to class, algebra book tucked under your arm and backpack fully stocked. Then you get this sinking feeling. People are looking at you funny, some bursting out in laughter and others pointing and calling their friends over when you pass. You start to worry. Then the panic sets in: *Do I have something on my face? Maybe my hair looks bad? Did I step in something gross? Or maybe someone taped a sign onto my back?* You look down to make sure that your outfit is OK, and much to your chagrin you find that you are … naked.

Lucky for you, that was just a dream. But if you are getting ready to enter high school, these anxieties are all too familiar.

High school is great. But the first few weeks (or months) of freshman year can be daunting. You have new teachers to get in synch with, new confusing social dynamics to work out, and new jam-packed hall-ways to navigate. You're also in the middle of a huge transition from adolescence to adulthood. It's all kind of scary. But it doesn't have to be.

Want to know how to assimilate into your new social kingdom? Avoid eating lunch alone on the first day of school? Or make a boring class more fun? We are four teenagers who were once freshmen ourselves, and we are going to tell you the stuff that no one told us—though we *wish* they had. Divided into three sections—Social Advice, Academic Advice, and Practical Advice—*Been There, Survived That* is your complete roadmap through your first year of high school. It includes tips on everything from how to deal with failure and survive group projects to how to make up good excuses for teachers and fake sick days. We even share our own freshman year horror stories so you won't feel so bad if you do accidentally show up to school naked (though that's not advised).

Cafeteria food is scary, but freshman year doesn't have to be. Just grab your books, your makeup, your skateboard, or whatever else you might need and get ready to learn the inner workings of high school. And hang on. Our book is pretty tame, but your year is bound to be one wild ride.

Joe Pinsker is a native of San Carlos, a suburb of San Francisco. He is a junior at Menlo School and enjoys reading books and magazines, writing essays and music reviews, and pondering the nature of humanity as he listens to eclectic music. He loves waking up on rainy mornings, laughing about odd things, and eating Indian food.

Hannah Shr is a San Francisco native who has grown up all her life with people trying to (unsuccessfully) guess her ethnicity. She is Chinese and Jewish, speaks Mandarin and Hebrew, and is an avid world traveler. She is a senior in the Creative Writing Department at San Francisco School of the Arts, and has published several poems in the *Umalut* literary journal and the Betsy Franco anthology *Falling Hard*. She likes body piercing, driving, laughing, avocados, and the color yellow.

Carolyn Hou is a native San Franciscan and a senior at Gateway High School. She really likes dill pickles, fluorescent colors, and journalism. She really hates long walks on the beach, soft grapes, and musicals. Her heroic icon is Pippi Longstocking.

Maxfield Peterson is an aspiring poet and author. He is a sophomore in the Creative Writing Department at San Francisco School of the Arts. When he's not doing homework, writing, or hanging out with his friends, he's cycling in nearby Marin. He loves the city that surrounds him and uses it for inspiration in his writing.

Max was the only one who was actually a freshman during the time the book was being written. He is glad to have been able to contribute recent firsthand knowledge of freshman year angst. He is also glad to be a sophomore.

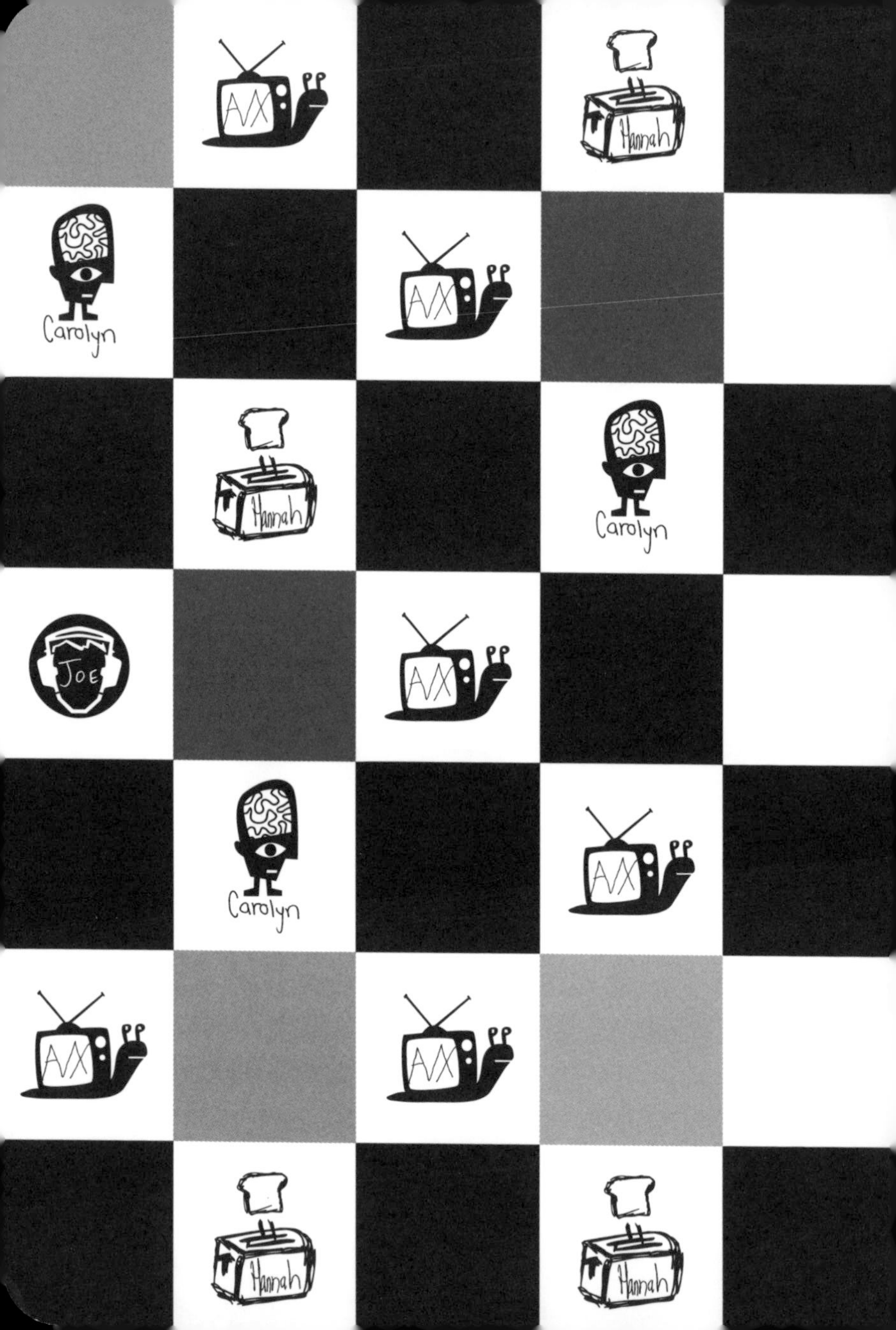
Hannah
Carolyn
Hannah
Carolyn
JOE
Carolyn
Hannah
Hannah

SOCIAL ADVICE

Be Aware of First Impressions

New year, new school, new life. Time to leave all your inhibitions at the door and go crazy, right? Wrong!!! First impressions count more than you think and, although you may be curious about the infamous "wild" life of high school, don't simply let go and do foolish things. Think about it—this is your chance to establish a whole new identity for yourself. Instead of becoming known as that girl who gets plastered and hooks up with everybody just because she can't control how much she drinks, or that show-off guy who broke his leg while doing some ridiculous skateboard stunt, earn a reputation as that "chill freshman," that "really nice girl," or that "funny guy."

You do not have to be a goody-two-shoes or anything. Just be smart about the choices you make. It's better to choose who you hang out with, as opposed to having those decisions made for you because you started off by doing lame things.

Top 5 Ways **NOT** to Make a Good Impression on a New Person

1	Spit in your palm before offering it for a handshake.
2	Laugh nervously and uncontrollably during your first conversation.
3	Slap them on the rear.
4	Come to school reading *World of Warcraft* strategy guides with chapter titles like "How to Improve Your Elf's Sex Life."
5	Use expressions like "ill," "savage," and "wicked" at least once in every sentence.

Don't Make Assumptions

That guy with the knee-high socks, oversize glasses, and headgear—you just want to call him a geek. How could you not? With that lab coat and the beakers, he's just asking for it, really. But before you go and make assumptions, step back for a moment and try to see that this guy could actually be any number of things. Just because someone dresses like a geek (or a jock, or a goth, or a hipster) doesn't mean they're truly one at heart. And besides, what does it even mean to be a jock, a goth, or a hipster? Does it define how good a friend you are? Or even what kind of TV you like to watch?

The great thing about people is that they can always surprise you and turn out to be exactly the opposite of who you thought they were. Wait till you really get to know someone before you decide what they are like or what kinds of things they are into. And don't be surprised when that future chemist takes off his lab coat to take your spot on the JV football team.

Freshman Year
SURVIVAL STORIES

Hannah

"It was probably the first few days of school, and I was a new freshman. Class had already started, and I ran to the bathroom to go pee. As I entered the bathroom I looked around—black walls and no mirrors. 'Well, I guess this is a public school,' I sighed to myself, more accustomed to the white, squeaky-clean bathrooms of my private middle school. I entered one of the stalls and went pee. As I came out I found the principal standing there—using one of the urinals!

"'I think you're in the wrong bathroom,' he said very politely. I felt a wave of humiliation wash over me, and I sank into my sweatshirt. What a fabulous way to start off freshman year!"

Work Out a Lunch Plan

No matter your gender, you don't want to wind up like Lindsay Lohan in *Mean Girls*, eating lunch all alone in the bathroom on the first day of school. No one talks about it when they prep you for high school, but eating lunch alone is really the pits. What you need is a lunch plan.

During one of your classes, ask that funny girl next to you what she is doing for lunch. Or look to see if your school has any clubs that gather during lunch so that you could meet like-minded people; or research whether any of the teachers open their rooms to students during lunch. You could also check down at the sports field and see if anyone has organized a game of soccer or is simply sunning themselves on the grass while they eat.

If all else fails, simply stroll into the cafeteria and look for someone you met that day and ask if you can sit with them. Don't worry about busting in on some already well-formed clique. It is only the beginning of school, and everybody is in the same position. Most of

these other kids are just like you, friendly, shy, interesting, and wanting a friend to eat with.

Top 5 Ways to Start a Conversation

1	"Hi. What's your name? My name is…" (This one works really well.)
2	Use common interests. "Hey, did you see that awesome episode of *Lost* last night?" or "My cat attacked my face last night. Do you like cats?"
3	Try compliments. "Those shoes are really cute! Where did you get them?" or "I really like all the hair on your arms."
4	Remark on things you find funny about the teacher or the school.
5	Ask someone what middle school they went to.

Meet New People

It can be terrifying at first, not knowing anybody in this new world of older, seemingly cooler people. You might be tempted to go in search of old friends and stick only to them for the rest of the year. But if you do, you're kind of missing the point.

The whole reason why we go to high school is to meet new people (and, OK, maybe learn a little). That shy kid sitting next to you in math class might wind up being the coolest person—or that girl you never talked to in middle school might one day be your best friend. Most of these kids are just as terrified and shy as you are, and you never know what kinds of friends you'll make until you try.

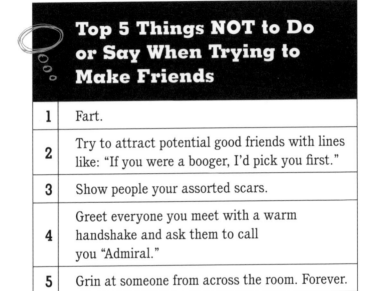

Top 5 Things NOT to Do or Say When Trying to Make Friends

1	Fart.
2	Try to attract potential good friends with lines like: "If you were a booger, I'd pick you first."
3	Show people your assorted scars.
4	Greet everyone you meet with a warm handshake and ask them to call you "Admiral."
5	Grin at someone from across the room. Forever.

Don't Take Things Personally

Freshman year can feel a lot like a poker game: One minute you have a sense that you are doing great and have all the friends you need, and the next minute it seems like you are losing — and all your friends have vanished. But, like in poker, the key to survival is to just hang back and not get too freaked out. The social universe will balance itself out, eventually.

When you enter high school, tons of doors open up for new friendships. But when people are making a lot of new friends, they sometimes neglect their old ones. If you feel like you're getting pushed aside by your old buddies, try not to take it as a personal attack or a sign that they no longer want to be friends (and be sensitive if *you* are the one wanting to let go a little bit).

For instance, it can be really disorienting when your best friend since third grade starts eating lunch somewhere else — you've known each other since …

forever. But your friend's behavior probably has very little to do with you. Maybe he's wanting to expand his own circle of friends. Or he might even feel weird around the new people you're hanging out with. It's important to remember that, whatever the reason, it's not your fault or his. People drift apart in high school, and sometimes they drift back together.

Change might not always feel good, but you'll eventually realize that things happen for a reason. Everything somehow falls into place. So try not to worry. Friends come and go, and losing and gaining friends is all part of the experience of growing up, becoming an adult, and ... surviving high school.

Be Careful Who You Trust

It's fascinating how your words have a way of finding their way to the very ears you didn't want them to. You know the game telephone? Well, the spreading of secrets works something like that. When you tell someone a secret about someone else, it's probably not going to stop there. And by the time this little secret reaches the ears of the other person, and it will, you can trust that through its many transporters it will have become significantly harsher and exaggerated. So what to do?

Sometimes you just have to tell someone something, like how you can't stand Daniel ever since he messed around with your ex-girlfriend. Or whatever. But before telling anyone anything, ask yourself the following questions about your proposed confidant.

1. Is this person a big source of gossip?

2. Do they have any connections to people you wouldn't want to hear this little secret?

3. And (the big question) do you trust this person?

Of course, it's also good to learn how to stay quiet. Friends can be good confidantes, and you should talk to them, but with really personal things that involve another person at school, you have to be extra careful. Secrets do get out. And once that happens, there's nothing you can do to take them back.

Learn How to Handle Being Messed With

At some point in everyone's life, they are messed with in some way, whether it's being made fun of or put in an embarrassing situation. The key to coping is knowing how to deal with these awkward moments.

It sucks to get teased, but even if your feelings are hurt, it's best not to let them show. One tactic is to just walk away and take a breather before you say something idiotic and make yourself look foolish. In general, acting on your impulses when you're angry will leave you even more embarrassed and probably regretting what you said. If you can't walk away (you are stuck in class or are with a group of people), keep your cool. If you stay calm, then whoever is being mean will look stupid.

It's also important to not take things too seriously. In most cases when someone makes you feel bad, they are just power tripping and don't even mean the things they're saying. Seniors and upperclassmen have better things to do than to focus on making your life hell; you are out of their thoughts 10 seconds after they tease you, and you should forget about it, too.

You may be tempted to tell a parent that you are being taunted, but that often only makes matters worse because then the whole school knows your mom is involved. Of course, if it gets *really* bad, you have no choice but to tell an adult (never put yourself in danger because of pride or fear).

Learning to deal with people you don't like is one of the most annoying facts of life. But it's still something we have to learn. High school is about growing into adulthood and you have to start to develop and manage real relationships with friends and enemies alike.

Carolyn

Get to Know the Upperclassmen

If you feel intimidated by older students, keep in mind that the almighty seniors were once fresh meat as well. They, too, walked the halls in fear and hid their lunch money when the older kids passed by. Now that they are older, the upperclassmen try to make you feel inferior, acting like they own the school and as if you are walking on their land.

But your school belongs to everyone, and just because you are younger, doesn't mean you have to do everything they say, like give them your chow mein at lunch or do their homework at night. If you stand up for yourself and don't avoid them at all costs, upperclassmen will begin to respect you more. The best thing to do is to find common ground with juniors and seniors, so you can actually be their friends instead of foes. Join clubs, take classes, and play sports with them, and make an effort to connect by any means. There's no rule that freshmen and seniors can't hang out — all you need is a basic level of understanding and some respect.

Top 6 Ways NOT to Try and Befriend a Senior

1	Offer to become their indentured servant in exchange for a weekly ride to In 'N' Out Burger.
2	Bake them cookies and ask them to be your friends.
3	Sit on the hood of their cars and wait for them after class.
4	Call their home phone repeatedly even though they never gave you their number.
5	Copy their haircut and wardrobe.
6	Constantly remind them that your PSAT score is higher than their SAT score.

When in Rome...

We've all heard it a million times: Be yourself, express yourself, don't be afraid of what others say or think. And, in general, it's good advice. But that doesn't mean you need to blast through the halls in a neon-green polyester miniskirt with thick yellow eyeliner streaming down your cheeks on the first day of school. The last thing you want to do is isolate yourself, which is easy to do freshman year when everyone is so freaked out by all of the new people around them.

There are plenty of ways to express your own tastes without alienating the whole world. And it's even OK to blend in a little at the very beginning of high school. This doesn't mean you should ditch your personality (see page 30), or do anything you don't want to, it just means that you should be open to taking part in the new culture around you. Sure, your real friends won't care what kind of clothes you wear once they get to know you—but these people don't know you yet! Give everyone some time to ease in to your sense of style. As they say: When in Rome, do as the Romans do.

Freshman Year
SURVIVAL STORIES   Hannah

"It was a sunny day and I was feeling daring. I wore a tiny hot-pink miniskirt to school. Nobody thought that it looked bad or ugly, but I did get many remarks about just how short the skirt was. The day had ended and I was walking out of the quad to go home. Not a usual skirt wearer, I jumped up and began to climb the concrete ramp adjacent to the stairs. As I jumped down my skirt flew up, flashing my butt to everyone standing behind me. I tried to pretend I didn't know what had happened and beelined it out of there."

Carolyn

Get Out
of the House

It's a Friday night after a long week of boring lectures, rotting school lunches, and an inhumane load of homework, and you're sitting at home at your computer, checking to see if maybe, just maybe, someone has sent you a MySpace comment. If this sounds all too familiar, then you have a problem.

You should be out of the house, meeting new people and having fun. In two days you'll be back to the same old routine of loud teachers and your cafeteria's infamous "surprise meat." Treasure your weekend time and use it wisely, which means trying to create a social life for yourself that is more than just playing Scrabble with your family or organizing your teachers' bookshelves. Sign up for clubs, go to social events like dances or festivals, and put yourself out there! It's not always easy to get out on the scene and challenge your comfort zone, but it always pays to try. Hey, you never know — the cashier who just sold you candied corn at your high school's Halloween festival could turn out to be your new best friend.

Freshman Year
SURVIVAL STORIES JOE

"During freshman year, a bunch of my friends and I were hanging out at school in an old room that we found. It had comfy couches and weird chairs that were shaped like hands. In the room, we found a box full of some random objects, the funniest of which was a large rabbit suit that I found fit me perfectly. After much encouragement, I donned the rabbit suit and went to lunch in the cafeteria. It was hard not to laugh at the reactions I got, but keeping quiet was extremely valuable in the end. After a fun trip to the cafeteria, I shed my rabbit disguise and along with it my temporary ability to make people laugh without even saying anything. From this experience I learned that you can easily make the most out of a routine activity in high school by spicing things up a bit. Especially with a bunny suit."

Don't Undergo a Total Personality Overhaul

Sometimes when we are around new people, we unconsciously change in an attempt to fit in. A little assimilation is natural (see page 26), and even good, but altering your whole personality can prevent you from meeting new people you might really connect with and get you stuck with people you have nothing in common with. Trying to be someone you are not for four years will make you uncomfortable and unhappy. It's a sucky way to experience high school.

So, wear what you feel comfortable in, play your kind of sports, and listen to the music you like, even if no one else likes it. Don't be afraid to say "I don't like this song," or "Everyone might be wearing those jeans, but they are still ugly." It is way cooler to be honest and have your own taste than simply to agree with the crowd. And while it sounds cheesy, being honest about everything you do will not only make you happier, but also help you find friends that you may keep for life.

Freshman Year
SURVIVAL STORIES
Carolyn

"As a freshman, I was shy to try new things and step out of my comfort zone. I hadn't been kissed or been on a real date yet, while my friends were already on their fourth boyfriends and teaching me what 'second base' meant. I still wasn't sure how to approach boys (and stop myself from turning a very dark shade of pink when I did), but I also wanted to venture out and start meeting new people.

"Finally, a classmate started talking to me more through email, AIM, and the phone. He seemed to have a sudden interest in me, and I had secretly had a tiny crush on him for months. I decided to take a risk and let my guard down, and we ended up talking every day and hanging out a lot. I was so comfortable with him that eventually we started to just date without him ever asking me the official 'Will you be my girlfriend?' question that every girl wants to hear. I've been dating him for a year now, and it's going great!"

Your Friends Are Dating— and You're Not!

When a good friend suddenly gets a girlfriend or boyfriend, it can really throw you off guard. Instead of having great conversations and doing cool things with him or her, you find yourself becoming a third wheel who sits on the couch, stares blankly into the TV, and gets frustrated at the wasted time spent watching these two losers lip wrestle. Maybe you even feel kind of inadequate or jealous. Or like you'd better start dating—and fast. You're not sure whether they're too early or you're too late, but you do know that you feel left out.

Don't worry. Your time will come. Everyone starts dating at different times. If you are late, it's not because you're shy or unattractive. It's just taking you more time than your friend to find someone you have chemistry with.

Jumping into a relationship as fast as you can just so you can feel like you're on par with your dating friends won't help the situation. You'll probably just find yourself being jostled around by a shallow obligation. Finding the right person at the right time is part of the process. In the meantime, hang out with some other single friends and give your coupled friends some space. And if they've really gone off the deep end, have them read the next page.

Top 5 Reasons It's Better to Be Single

1	You don't have to worry about commitments.
2	You never feel guilty about hanging out with your friends.
3	You won't be known as so-and-so's boyfriend/girlfriend.
4	You have more free time (and money).
5	You don't have to worry about shaving.

Don't Ditch Your Friends for a New GF/BF

Igh school arrives with a trail of homework, hysteria—and hormones. Naturally, you are going to start going on dates, hooking up, and maybe even getting close to a boyfriend or girlfriend. Yeah, it's fun, it feels good, and you feel like all you want to do is hang out with that special person. But there is always another angle you're not seeing. In this case, it's probably your friend's.

Your relationship with your girlfriend or boyfriend may be great, but that doesn't mean it's OK to ignore your old friends, even if you are doing it subconsciously. They have been there for you through everything: good times, boredom, sadness, and major life disappointments. Don't forget that they exist! Stay aware of the way you're dividing your time between your new BF or GF and your old buddies, and make sure your friends always know how important they are to you. Relationships from freshman year rarely last, even if it some-

times seems like they will go on forever. And when you
start having romantic trouble, you'll need someone to
help you through the rough patches, or the breakup.

Top 6 Pickup Lines to NEVER Use

1	"Are you lost? Because heaven is a long way from here."
2	"I only have 3 months to live and I'm a virgin. Maybe you can help?"
3	"Are you from Tennessee? Because you're the only 10 I see!"
4	"Excuse me, have you seen my library card? Because I'm checking you out."
5	"Are you tired? Because you've been running through my mind all day."
6	"Chicks dig me. I wear purple underwear."

BEEN THERE

Cultivate a Couple of Good Friends

Sometimes it can seem hard to balance your social life with your academic one. Although good grades are key, friends are equally important. And that perfect A that you spent all your afternoons studying for does not count as a friend. Over the next four years, you're bound to have some problems—big problems—and although you'll be able to get through some of them on your own, you're going to need some good friends to talk to about things, whether it's family problems, or a not-so-satisfying report card or an ugly relationship. So, even on the first day of school, be on the lookout for people you think you could really spend some time and connect with. John Lennon said it best when he sang, "I get by with a little help from my friends."

Freshman Year
SURVIVAL STORIES

Carolyn

"Wanting to bring back my childhood, I bought a vintage 1990s lunch box with the Simpsons on the cover as a way to take my lunch to school. I showed it off for weeks and then, one day, packed a delicious almond butter and honey sandwich inside, along with a hardboiled egg.

"I wasn't up to eating the hardboiled egg, so I left it in my lunch box in my locker. I ended up leaving that lunch box in my locker, which I share with three friends, for a few weeks. I just never got around to lugging the huge box back home. Finally, after my friends started wondering where the mysterious stinky cheese smell was coming from, I decided I had to man-up and admit it was my lunch box. After about four different washes of my lunch box in the lunchroom, I finally got the stench out. But my locker never smelled the same way again, and my friends won't let me live it down."

JOE
Carolyn
JOE
A/X
Carolyn
JOE
A/X
Hannah
Carolyn
JOE
Hannah
Carolyn

ACADEMIC ADVICE

Carolyn

Make a Game Plan

There is nothing worse than waiting until the very last month of your senior year to learn that you have to complete 150 community service hours, another course of Humanities, 60 PE credits, and Photography II (when you still haven't taken Photography I). Suddenly, college seems very far away. So how can you guarantee that you'll graduate on time?

You need to find out all of the requirements for graduation, from how many PE credits you need to the required amount of extracurricular classes. This is the time to pay a visit to your guidance counselor, or any of the white-haired advisers at school who know something about anything. They will tell you what you need to take and when.

As soon as you know your requirements, make a dedicated plan to start completing them. To do this, map out all of the classes you absolutely need to take for freshman, sophomore, junior, and senior year.

It's helpful to look at the big picture while planning. For instance, if you know that junior year will be very stressful because you'll be studying for the SATs, looking into colleges, and perhaps even taking AP classes, you might want to take one of your harder electives in your freshman or sophomore year.

Be sure to also research what specific requirements you need to apply to certain colleges and universities. Perhaps that private liberal arts school you're dying to go to requires three years of language instead of two. If you are unsure of what schools you want to apply to, it never hurts to take an extra class here or there in order to keep your options open. When you first start high school, you have a very long four years ahead—you don't want to make that five.

Carolyn

Tap Your Peer Resources

Should you take that math class taught by the math teacher with the blue-streaked hair who doesn't give much homework but gives hard tests? Or the one taught by the young nerd with pocket protectors who assigns loads of homework but never gives tests at all? Yes, parents and teachers are always offering advice, but the best way to find solutions to these types of conundrums is by asking siblings, cousins, friends, and classmates who are a couple of years older than you. First, they're closer to your age and better understand your perspective. And, more important, they've been through exactly what you're going through. Whether you are trying to figure out which teacher you should request for biology, or if you should take the English honors course, or even where the best restaurant around school is, these are the people who can give you the scoop.

And remember: While it's good to get advice, you don't always have to take it. People will have different tastes. You might realize that the extremely strict biology teacher that everyone hates is actually a funny guy — and a really good teacher.

Freshman Year
SURVIVAL STORIES
Hannah

"One day in chemistry class, I was sitting next to my friend Jelli at a table. Class was so boring that we decided we just had to devise a plan to make mischief. We noticed we were sitting next to power outlets and decided that the next Tuesday would be smoothie day. I brought the blender; she brought the ice cream and fruit. We set the blender up and plugged it into the wall just as class began. We then proceeded to make smoothies, pushing the Blend button each time the teacher would pause in his lecture. He was not amused. In the end it all worked out: Our smoothies were tasty and our chemistry teacher was quite irritated. Mission accomplished."

Be Cool to Your Teachers

Despite what you may think, teachers are people too, and they deserve to be treated nicely—not like sadistic psychopaths. This doesn't mean you should kiss up to get better grades (see page 62), just that you should practice common courtesy.

An easy way to show respect is to say "Hello" when you come into class or when you pass in the halls. It's even better if you can figure out if they prefer "Sup?" to the classic "Good morning!" Also, try not to create distractions during class. Basically, you want to interact with a teacher as you would with any other human being who has emotions.

If you respect your teachers, they'll start to respect you—and that means they'll probably start to see you as a more serious student. And that certainly can't hurt your grades.

Top 10 Ways to Get Teachers to Really DISLIKE You

1	Stiff arm all the would-be answerers in class so that your teacher can see that you know the answer to *every* question.
2	Imitate your teacher's style of clothing.
3	Use lame pickup lines on them.
4	Set their desktop image to an embarrassing photo you took of them, in which they are not-so-discreetly picking their nose.
5	Start telling your friends and other teachers that you're having an affair with your teacher.
6	Repeat everything they say during class in an obnoxious voice.
7	TP their house.
8	Send them cute e-cards on every occasion.
9	Address them as "doll."
10	Correct them constantly in front of the class.

Play Well With Others

High school introduces you to some of life's crappier points: sleep deprivation, social nightmares … and group projects gone wrong. No matter how much you complain, your teacher will assign group projects and, yes, that means you have to work with other people. Group projects don't have to be the rotten experiences they can easily turn into. Here are some tips that will help.

1. Divide the workload equally.

Keep in contact with other group members to make sure everyone's pulling their own weight (that includes you, too).

2. Keep personality type in mind.

Working together is not just about completing a project. It's about learning to deal with all types of personalities — from slackers to anal-retentive worka-holics. Try to split up the work according to people's abilities and personality types—meaning don't give the most important part of the project to someone who is absent four days a week.

3. Handle things maturely.

If a group member isn't following through, don't go straight to your teacher and whine. First talk (nicely) to other people in your group and see what's holding things up. If you decide to approach a teacher because you think your grade is going to suffer, try not to point fingers. Just maturely explain the situation and ask for advice on the best way to handle it.

4. Learn to work with people you don't like.

It's no fun when the teacher assigns you to work with Halitosis Kid. Still, it's best not to get dramatic or grimace (even if his breath makes you want to vomit). Teachers are looking for cooperation; they want you to make an effort to work as a group. Just dole out a few breath mints and deal.

Carolyn

Get Organized

Are you incessantly shuffling through hundreds of pieces of paper from seven different classes looking for that one particular homework assignment that just *has* to be turned in today only to realize that you left it at home — again? The old "my baby sister ate my homework" isn't going to work this time (or ever, for that matter). The only way to prevent this from happening again is to get organized! Here are some tips.

1. Invest in a daily planner.
Use it to write down social events, homework, birthdays, and hot dates.

2. Keep your textbooks in one place.
This way, you won't lose them.

3. Check your lockers.
Every day at the end of school, make sure you have all the papers and books you might need for homework.

4. Clean out your backpack.

Rotting food and crumpled papers can get stuck at the bottom of your backpack, which makes things really hard to find. Clean out your backpack once a week for a good, fresh start.

5. Carry less stuff.

Take home only the homework and books you need to instead of carrying everything all the time and bearing all that unnecessary weight. You can even take pictures of homework pages with a digital camera and look at those on the computer instead of bringing the whole heavy textbook home.

In general, getting organized can only mean one thing: making your life easier. And that's something worth spending some time on.

Find a Study Spot at Home

Our parents frequently advise us to separate work from play, and there's a reason. When you multitask while you do your homework, you do everything with only a very low level of efficiency, as opposed to just doing one thing very well.

To do schoolwork, it's best if you can create a calm, fairly quiet atmosphere that maximizes your efficiency. That means that you should shut down your laptop (unless you need it), turn off your music, clear your desk of all of its worthless crap (no, that doesn't include homework), and close the door.

Getting your study space rid of any distractions (including Internet capability) can be hard at first, but it will enable you to finish your homework faster, leaving you more time to give your full attention to important activities like trolling YouTube and chatting on IM.

Freshman Year
SURVIVAL STORIES

"One time in freshman year, I delayed turning in an English essay. I actually did write this paper only two days after it was due, but the fear of handing it in late prevented me from turning it in to my teacher. I decided to sleep on it. Then sleep on it again. And again. And I slept on that decision for two weeks until the saying 'better late than never' finally came to mind. I came into class while the teacher was out at lunch and snuck the paper into his 'turned-in' bin. Now I still can't say for sure what happened, but that paper was returned to me three days later with an A, and I thank the demi-god of academia everyday for what must have been a mistake."

Identify
Some Allies

In order to survive academically, you'll definitely need some allies. Look for classmates you can count on for homework help, to ask questions about an assignment, or to study with for a test. They don't have to be your best friends, but it's best if they're people you don't hate with a passion. You can choose them as soon as the first day of freshman year. Find a person who would make a good study buddy and swap contact information.

Now if you have a question that you forgot to ask a teacher or if you're having trouble with an assignment, you can ring up your newfound buddy and fire away. You can even share notes with your allies and check (not copy) each other's work.

Keep on good terms with your allies and make sure that they know you are also there to help. And try to find backups in all of your classes in case your number one ally gets the flu the same day as you.

Top 7 Indicators of a Good Ally

1	They actually take notes.
2	They're cute.
3	Their water cycle environmental project diorama was freaking amazing.
4	They built a replica of the human digestive system using only canned peaches, toothpicks, and slabs of raw meat.
5	They've memorized the periodic table of the elements—both forward and backward.
6	They'd pee on you if you were stung by a jellyfish.
7	They demonstrate a clear understanding of the difference between allies and "stalker buddies."

BEEN THERE SURV

Learn How to Fake It

Telling the truth is great. But if you want to get through high school alive, you're going to need to know how to tell the occasional white lie. So why not learn how to do it well?

The best strategy for lie-crafting is to try to see things through the teacher's eyes. Imagine for a moment that you are old Mrs. Peterson, and you've just spent the last 12 hours slaving over reports and essays. The last thing you want to hear is that someone didn't do the assignment that you so carefully made up because they were "too distracted by the football game."

When you fib, you need to connect with the teacher as much as you can. Look confident, yet sincere and slightly regretful. Don't approach your teacher's desk with your knees buckling and perspiration dripping from your forehead, as you slowly mutter some terrible excuse under your breath.

To become a better fibber, rehearse your excuse on the way to class, and make sure it's good. ("My dog ate it" or "My grandmother died. Again." are *not* good excuses.) Then, approach the desk slowly. "Hey Mr. X, I did my homework, but my printer wasn't working. I can e-mail it to you right when I get home. I'm *really* sorry."

You may have to spend some time working out the tone and cadence, but with practice your delivery will soon be convincing. And don't use the same excuse with the same teacher twice. If they bought it the first time, be thankful. You probably won't get that lucky the second time around.

Learn How to Deal With Failure

Unless you're a genius, you *will* get lower than an A from time to time—maybe much lower. Keep in mind that one D$^+$ doesn't mean you've failed in life. It just means that, well, you had absolutely no idea what the test was about. It's best if you can laugh at your brainlessness on problem 10, or at least chuckle a little about it, instead of going online immediately to find out which jobs don't require a high school diploma.

But now that you're in high school, which is far more challenging than middle school, academic failures *will* happen more often. Instead of locking yourself in a dark, cold room for a month without access to food or water, just get over it and move on. If you do, it'll be easier to deal with bigger failures in the future when you truly screw up.

Top 8 Ways NOT to Deal With Failure

1	Never go to school again.
2	Punch a wall so it can feel the same pain you do.
3	Defiantly yell "*not fair!*" in a teacher's face.
4	Publicly cry and draw massive amounts of attention to yourself.
5	Start a new life in Mexico.
6	Drop-kick your baby brother as a symbol of your frustration.
7	Slash your teacher's tires.
8	Join a cult.

Carolyn + Joe

Learn to Deal With Stress and Burnout

Slouched in your chair, you stare blankly at your computer screen, which is the only thing lighting up your room. You watch the cursor blink, and your mind isn't anywhere in particular. Your mouth hangs open, and drool slowly drips from your mouth. It's a bad scene and it's only the end of the first month of school. What happened? It's called burnout. Basically, you overdid it.

The best way to avoid burnout is to allow time every day for TV, napping, or simply petting your chinchilla while staring at the ceiling. Even a five-minute break from sitting at a computer can work wonders.

If you are already burned out — or just incredibly stressed — the best thing to do is to take a break from schoolwork. Meditate, do yoga, read, listen to your favorite band, play music, draw, shop, drive, sleep, eat, or dance around in your underwear to the Spice Girls. Do whatever speaks to you. Or do nothing — just spend some time alone, lounging around in your pajamas or sitting in the sun. Even when it seems like you just have to finish that paper or study for that test, your own sanity and well being should always be your number one priority.

Top 5 Ways NOT to De-Stress

1	Study more—you'll eventually get used to it.
2	Eat until you can't eat any more.
3	Constantly tell yourself that sleeping is a sign of weakness.
4	Sniff whiteboard markers between classes.
5	Put your head between your legs and scream like a banshee.

Carolyn

Get Help

Have you felt dumbstruck by the thought of solving the quadratic equation? Do you not understand why DNA helicase is important to copy genes? Don't worry, we've all been there. We've all felt as if we were reading the same words over and over (and over and over and over) again, never grasping the concept. If $e = mc^2$, then that must mean Einstein is a genius and you're a dolt? Nooo.

Sometimes people take more time to understand concepts and need lots of repetition to understand the material. If that's you, don't worry. Many schools offer free tutoring so that people can go over past tenses in Spanish with you, help you revive your skills in long division, or even discuss Greek mythology. Many times, when you get one-on-one help, a lightbulb will suddenly turn on.

If there aren't any tutoring options at your school, ask your parents or teachers for some extra help, or go to your local library to see if someone there can lend you a hand. It's better to get the help as soon as you need it so you don't fall even further behind in classes.

Freshman Year
SURVIVAL STORIES

"The first quarter of my freshman year I was clueless about how teachers would grade me and what the consequences of each grade would be. I struggled in my algebra class throughout the entire first grading period and somehow emerged with my first F ever. I couldn't believe it.

"Eventually, I told my parents. I asked for help, and we called a math tutor. The next grading period I glided through unscathed, getting a solid 3.5 GPA. This first dose of high school was actually one of the best things that could have happened to me. It made me realize that you almost never get anything right the first time around, and that as long as you build from your failures, there's nothing to worry about."

Don't Kiss Up

OK, so you're aware that the capital of Kazakhstan is Astana, and you also know that the difference between African and Indian Elephants is their ear sizes. However, any classmate or teacher, Kazakhstani, African, Indian, or otherwise, doesn't want to hear you consistently reel off a chain of facts and leave other students in the dust. No one likes a teacher's pet. And besides, you don't want to set the expectation that you know everything in class: The day *will* come when you get an answer wrong.

A quick way to shed the image of a teacher's pet or to avoid it entirely is to step back and let Trevor or Matt handle the next question, even though you're sure Trevor couldn't find Kazakhstan with a map of Central Eurasia in his hand, and that Matt is still mastering what sound an elephant makes. It's fine to answer questions, but teachers also admire a little bit of restraint. So every once in a while, hold back a little—it's always better to be the quiet, wise sage than to be the anxious dweeb who raises a hand before the teacher even finishes their question.

Freshman Year
SURVIVAL STORIES

Carolyn

"Freshman year of high school, four friends and I were known as the 'weird locker girls.' Why? Simply because everyday at lunch, before school, after school, and during passing, we would huddle around one locker in the main hallway. It was a place where we claimed our territory and giggled and gossiped about everything from cute boys to girls we didn't like. Later on, we noticed that rumors were flying around about us. People seemed to know who we had crushes on, or what we did last weekend with our parents, or other things that are too horrible to tell. How did they know this stuff? They had been listening to us from the bathrooms, which surrounded both sides of our lockers! Let's just say, the boy I liked then didn't find out I liked him quite the way I had intended him to."

Act Like
a Freshman

With all of these new extracurricular opportunities everywhere, you may find your schedule getting full. But if your weekday nights start consisting of volleyball practice, mathletes, Gay Straight Alliance meetings, judo practice, and SAT prep, you need to get a grip. If there was ever a year to kick back, it's freshman year.

Take care of your schoolwork, pick up one or two after-school activities (tops!), and relax. And don't register for 30 AP classes sophomore year. It's good to start thinking about college, but it's also OK to remember that you *are* still in high school. You'll be better off doing the work actually allotted to you than spreading out your energy into unnecessary endeavors. Work on your social situation, pick up a new hobby, indulge in television, read good books, and do stuff with your friends. The reality is that this year is really a breeze. As for the upcoming ones (shudder), you'll need the all the energy you can muster.

Freshman Year
SURVIVAL STORIES

JOE

"Going into freshman year, I had a good amount of friends, but I also had three or four 'best friends,' who I was sure would stick with me for a while. But near the end of freshman year, one of my friends and I started having a lot of disagreements, and it was weird to see that happen after all we'd been through. The relationship only went downhill from there. We're juniors now and rarely talk to each other, and even when we do talk, it's pretty awkward. This taught me that by the time you become an upperclassman, even though it may be hard to believe, you will probably have lost one of your best friends and made a new one. I was surprised to find how much I'd changed since freshman year, but I guess that's one of the things about high school that you just get used to."

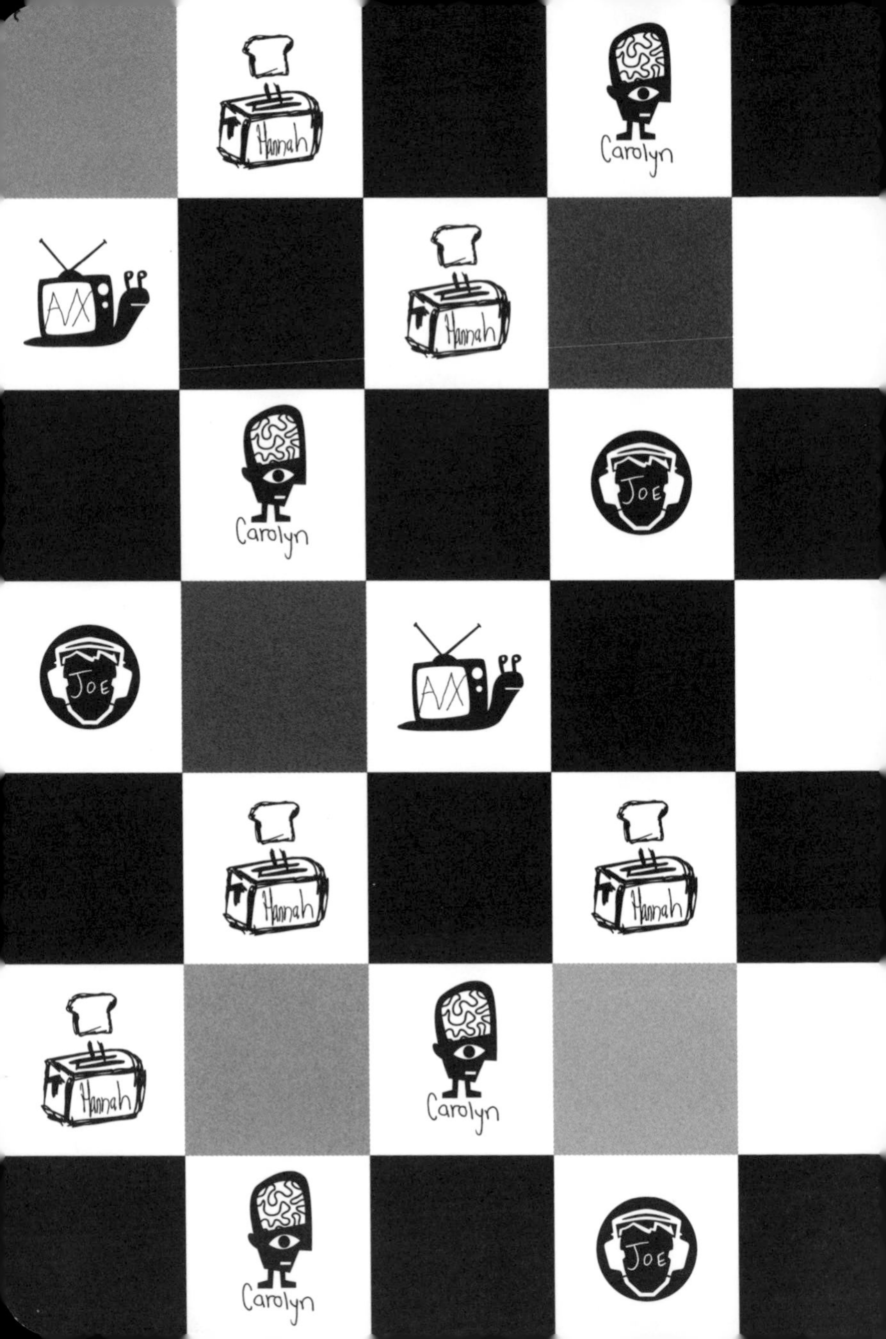

PRACTICAL ADVICE

Carolyn

Know the Landscape

etween keeping your shoelaces tied, trying not to lose your schedule, and struggling to get to your classes on time while avoiding the senior jocks who think they own the place, your first day of school is sure to be stressful. If you don't want to make it even more stressful, arrive with a decent understanding of the new place you'll be coming to five times a week for ten months, multiplied by four.

Scope out your high school—and the areas around it—before high school even begins. Know the bus routes that will take you to school from your home, or to school from the library, or from school to your boyfriend's or girlfriend's house. Know where the cafeteria is *and* where you can get cheap Chinese food when you have off-campus lunch. Know which café or burger joint will provide the best ambiance for you to cram before a huge test. And, perhaps most important, find out where the bathrooms are, inside and outside of school.

Knowing where you are and where you are going during the first few weeks of high school will help you retain enough brain cells to deal with meeting new people, getting on the good sides of your teachers, and checking out your cute new classmates.

Top 8 Things to Always Have on You at School

1	Money
2	Daily planner
3	Cell phone
4	Extra pens, pencils, and paper
5	Public transport maps and schedules
6	ID (student ID, driver's license)
7	Coat or sweater
8	Keys

Watch Your Stuff

aybe you went to a middle school where you could leave your backpack alone in the hallway and two hours later it would still be there, untouched. If so, you were lucky. (If not, you'll be better prepared for what lies ahead.) Rich or poor, high school is a place where things go missing. It's not that the kids are necessarily bad, but leaving a backpack unattended with a $150 iPod dangling out of it is just not smart.

Bags and personal items are hard to keep track of, and even more so when you are distracted and in a new environment. After school, when you are hanging out with your friends in the hallways or running around in the courtyard, it's easy to forget that your backpack is still sitting all alone in front of the lockers or wherever you last stashed it. Always keep an eye on it, and make sure the place you leave it during lunch, gym, or dance class is safe. If you keep everything in a locker, invest in a good lock and use it.

Freshmen tend to be targets for theft because they are usually coming from smaller, more intimate middle schools where everyone knows everyone and the "upperclassmen" are nervous 13-year-olds who are freaked out about high school as opposed to big 18-year-olds who drive and shave. Don't let the 18-year-olds go home with your iPod.

Make the Best of a Boring Class

Good grades are important, yes. But there will be days when you just *cannot* pay attention in class or are bored to tears. Here are some small ways of dealing.

• Text message friends in other classes

Keep the phone on silent, of course.

• Write and pass notes

Passing the note without getting caught is half the thrill, so put some attention into learning to do this right. If you throw enough notes across the room, you can even develop a muscular throwing arm.

• Discreetly snooze

Try this during a movie or at a time when you won't be noticed. (If you are super tired during a class in which you *must* stay awake, try standing up or splashing water on your face.)

• **Draw**

This is the best way to get your creative juices flowing. If you don't know how to begin, try drawing fat little caricatures of everyone you know.

Just remember that if you're going to be obnoxious and not pay attention in class, don't be obvious about it. Give the teacher some respect and don't disrupt the lesson. Besides, if they catch you, you can kiss that A good-bye.

Take Sick (or Not-So-Sick) Days

That math test is today and you really didn't study, and your science project really should be a little more than that shabby poster-board over in the corner. Your head is starting to swell with stress and all you can think about is numbers and averages and grades. You haven't missed a day all semester. It might be time to get sick.

Once or twice a year, you're going to need to stay home from school, avoid the music everyone is telling you to face, kick back on your couch, take an unnecessary aspirin, and cough up enough of a storm that your parents will believe you. This is just what you need—and you know it. Slump into the deepest sanctums of your living room sofa and enjoy a little Jerry Springer, or any of that classic, trashy, all-American daytime TV that unemployed adults and fellow "sick" teens have come to know and love. Let the knowledge that the whole world is moving on without you relax your muscles and ease your stress.

If you're going to enjoy this day to the fullest, you have to make sure everything goes smoothly. In the morning when your mom shoves you awake, make an even bigger fuss than you usually do. Have a major coughing fit as you get out of bed, then fall back onto it and moan. Don't overdo it because then you'll end up in the doctor's office, and that's even worse. Instead, attempt to get up and go about your daily routine, but fail miserably. And wind up back in bed.

As long as you keep it to one or two of these little absences per year, it won't hurt you a bit. So never be afraid to just take the day off when you really need it. Your body — and your grades — will thank you.

Purge!

Maybe you have a special attachment to your beloved report on African swallows or your essay on *To Kill a Mockingbird*, but the truth is you won't look at the majority of your middle school work ever again. So there's really no point in holding on to every single test, paper, and index card you collected during the past three years. Starting high school is about starting over. You need to purge!

Purging means getting rid of stuff. It's not only a way to reduce clutter and help with organization, but symbolically it gives you a sense of starting anew. You can purge almost everything, except for reference materials that could come in handy next school year. So, how to get rid of all those worthless papers collected from your room, locker, and backpack?

Try these techniques:

- **Go the classic route and fold them into paper airplanes.**

- **Take the environmentally conscious path and recycle them.**

- **Toss your papers into the nearest fire (preferably in a fireplace).**

Once you're unburdened of all this crap from the past, you'll feel like a new person. And when your freshman year is over, do it again. In fact, invite over a group of friends and chuck your crap from freshman year together.

Carolyn

Read!

You might be thinking that the last thing you need to add to your list of things to do freshman year is extracurricular reading. But you shouldn't let the amount of (or type of) books you read at school turn you off to the idea of reading. Reading is great for many reasons. Not only does it help challenge your creativity and allow you to see how other people think, but it also helps you build your vocabulary and grammar skills, which will help you in every aspect of life. Getting lost in a good book is also a wonderful stress reducer. This doesn't mean you have to read *Macbeth* or the Bible to benefit from reading—in fact, you should just read things that you enjoy and can relate to. Grab the latest *Seventeen* or *Slap* magazine, *Mad* comics, or even young adult novels from your local library. Or spend some time scoping out your parents' bookshelves. Pick up books that sound interesting to you and read the first few pages. If you start to yawn, stop reading and pick up another. The reading you do for yourself should always be enjoyable!

Top 13 Books You Should Read, But Don't Read in School

1	*Franny and Zooey* by J. D. Salinger
2	*The Five People You Meet in Heaven* by Mitch Albom
3	*Running With Scissors* by Augusten Burroughs
4	*The Lovely Bones* by Alice Sebold
5	*The Shadow of the Wind* by Carlos Ruiz Zafón
6	*Angels & Demons* by Dan Brown
7	*The Perks of Being a Wallflower* by Stephen Chbosky
8	*Even Cowgirls Get the Blues* by Tom Robbins
9	*America (The Book)* by Jon Stewart
10	*A Million Little Pieces* by James Frey
11	*Bel Canto* by Ann Patchett
12	*Cat's Cradle* by Kurt Vonnegut, Jr.
13	*A Tree Grows in Brooklyn* by Betty Smith

BEEN THERE, SURVIVE THAT

Eat and Sleep

You wake up at 6 every morning, only to devour a few Pop Tarts, which you promptly wash down with a can of Red Bull. This isn't exactly the breakfast of champions. And what about your sleep schedule? Do you really think five hours a night will get you through the next year? You may be young, but you're not invincible.

Your new high school schedule may leave little time for good food decisions and even less time for sleeping. But it's important to remember that eating and sleeping really do affect your mood, your grades, and even your growth. When you don't eat and sleep properly, your memory is compromised, you're crankier, and your motivation gets drained. Try to eat a deli sandwich instead of chocolate for lunch and sleep for at least seven hours every night. Hopefully, your Pop Tarts and Red Bulls won't miss you too much.

Freshman Year
SURVIVAL STORIES   JOE

"One time during freshman year, I got my food in the cafeteria like always and stopped to get a tall cup of orange juice before sitting down. When I sat down, one of my friends started shaking the table and yelling 'Earthquake!' It was kind of funny for a little while — like about 4 seconds — and then it was just annoying. Soon, people started looking over towards our table to see what was going on. A few seconds later, the 'earthquake' increased in magnitude, and my cup of OJ toppled into my lap, leaving a nice big wet spot in my crotchal region. A few of the observers started clapping as was tradition when someone dropped a plate or glass in my cafeteria. Suffice it to say that, with the wet crotch and the scores of onlookers, it was a long walk from my table to the cafeteria door."

BEEN THERE, SURVIVED THAT

Carolyn

Stay Safe

Being new anywhere can make a person feel pretty vulnerable, but that's not a vibe you want to give off to people around you. Here are a few safety tips to get you through freshman year safely.

1. Look more confident than you feel.

When blowfish get scared, they get bigger. So, act like a blowfish. When people know you are vulnerable, they will take advantage of you, which can mean doing anything from taking your lunch money to stalking you.

2. Leave a sketchy situation.

It's always better to be safe than sorry. If you don't feel safe, or if you feel scared, then get out of the situation you are in as soon as possible. Trust your intuitions!

3. Travel in groups.

Emulate your preschool bathroom buddies system
(it does work!) because there is always safety in
numbers. Plus, you and your friends will also just feel
safer knowing that you are looking out for one another.

4. Don't look lost.

When you act like you know where you're going,
people will believe you know where you are going
and will be less likely to bother you. Of course, the
best way to not look lost, is to actually not be lost!
(See page 68.) Look at maps before you go places, call
transport agencies to see when your buses are coming,
and always have the number of a taxi on you. Bottom
line is that you should do whatever you need to do to
be safe.

Revamp Your Room

So you still have the same white wicker furniture and pink blankets in your room that you got when you were 7, a bin of Barbies (which are now taking up space in your closet), and a childhood desk that's not big enough for you to actually study at anymore. It's not healthy to be a teenager living in a kids room. This is a new time in your life—it's time to renovate! Paint your walls orange, buy leopard sheets, throw away your old toys! Redesign your room with a new ninth-grade sensibility, whatever that means to you. And if your parents are willing to pitch in a few dollars, use this time as an excuse to buy new stuff—like a more functional desk for your upcoming (torturous) high school workload. Stuck at getting started on your new room? Here are some hints to help.

• Re-arrange

Move your bed to a new place in your room. Shifting furniture can change the entire feel of a room, and the best part is it's free!

• Be daring

Buy things you've always wanted, but never had the chance to get. Maybe a beanbag chair, new curtains, or beads for the doorway. Or even a white shag carpet!

• Paint the walls

White walls can be soooo boring (and if you've had them a long time, they are also probably pretty dirty). Choose a favorite color, but not one that you will hate in three months.

• Post

Cover the walls with your favorite song lyrics, letters from friends, movie posters, stickers, and so on. Put up favorite photos or magazine clippings to make the room really yours. Like the Spice Girls? Infatuated with *Star Wars*? Who cares what other people think. Decorate however you like. It's *your* room.

BEEN THERE, SURVIVED THAT

Carolyn

Get a Job

What's worse than having a hot date but not being able to go because your parents won't give you the money to see the movie? This is a perfect reason to get a job — you need some financial independence.

Getting a job is a step toward proving that you are becoming a responsible man or woman. Jobs are great since you get to be away from school and home for a few hours a week while making some cash and learning new things. You'll meet people, get contacts and experience for jobs you might want to pursue later on in life, and learn how to monitor your own cash flow.

To find a job, you can go the traditional routes (apply for jobs at the mall), but you generally need to be 16 for those. You can also ask family members and friends if they know anyone who needs some help around the house or with their business.

Sure, not every high school job is going to be a thrill.
Maybe it's not that exciting to learn how to file,
make a nonfat iced caramel macchiato, or lick 1,000
envelopes in a row. But whatever you're doing, you're
learning something new and making money.

Top 6 Jobs NOT to Get

1	Babysitter of chatterbox 4-year-old.
2	Toilet maintenance manager at your local Indian restaurant.
3	Farm hand responsible for artificially inseminating a cow.
4	Guinea pig for a chemical weapons testing corporation.
5	Supervisor of committee on universal health care solutions for America.
6	Exotic pole dancer in a strip club your biology teacher frequents.

BEEN THERE, SURVIVED THAT

Find Your Calling—Get an Internship

Even though you are only just starting high school, freshman year can be a good time to try to find your calling in life. One way to do that is to search out a good internship in a field you think you might progress in.

An internship is usually an unpaid job, but it's in a more advanced and professional field than any paying job you could land at this age. You might pick up secretarial work at a law firm to learn about the legal system, or help maintain the local museum to learn more about art. The work is not always exciting, but the environment is what matters. Jobs like these can open up a lot of doors later, and take you one step closer to your career.

Most internships are unpaid, but others can bring in some money—without forcing you to slave in desert heat all day at a hot-dog stand listening to people jabber on about your high prices. Internships also look good on a college application, and it never hurts to give your future a little thought.

Internships range from small-time administrative work (like filing papers) to assisting in scientific research, teaching and constructing curriculum, or even working at your local zoo. Don't write anything off because it seems boring at first.

These positions are sometimes harder to find than ordinary high school jobs, and they're more competitive, but they give you a huge advantage in life. In 30 years, when you're helping support a family with a career that inspires and interests you, you'll look back and be glad you took that internship instead of (or in addition to) serving fries at the dingy McDonalds down the street.

Join a
Sports Team

Throughout high school, you'll probably start asking yourself some big "What-if?" questions: "What if the world ended tomorrow and I still hadn't yet run with the bulls in Pamplona, Spain?" or "What if I were being chased by several robot monkeys with swords and my legs suddenly stopped working?" Obviously, not all "What-if?" questions are meant to be answered, but if you find yourself asking, "What if I threw aside all my doubts and awkwardness and tried out for the soccer team?" you should listen to that inner voice.

High school is meant for trying new things. It's a time to step out of your comfort zone, which is just a nice way of saying, do something you are afraid to do, like try out for a school team. Maybe you don't think you're athletic enough, or fear that you'd be wasting your teammates' time with your lack of talent, or have always assumed that sports were just for the jocks. But you need to get past that. Not all high school sports are as competitive or rigorous as you think, and joining a team is about more than scoring goals or sinking baskets. It helps you build confidence and make new friends, and it offers a camaraderie that's hard to find in other extracurricular activities. Plus, it gets you into shape, which could never hurt your new high school social life, unless getting winded while walking to class or not being able to peel yourself off the couch suddenly becomes all the rage.

Get to Know Your Parents

Getting to know your parents may seem totally irrelevant to getting through freshman year, but it's not. Parents can be good friends, shoulders to lean on, and allies when the going gets a little tough. Learning that your parents are actual, bona fide people is also the first step to developing real relationships with them, which is important to your development as an adult. And cultivating an actual bond between you and your parent or guardian can also work in your favor! If your parents like and respect you, they will probably be more lenient and understanding when it comes to things like curfew, allowance, and so on.

It can be hard to get to know your parents—they can be weird, mean, unfair, irrational, and even smell a little funny—but it is well worth it. Though they are from a different generation, they were once our age and can relate to most of our experiences. Besides, they really want to be there for you.

To get closer to them, explore things you have in common. Do both you and your mother love watching old movies? Or maybe you and your pop both love sailing? Whatever it is that you and your parents can connect about, from peanut butter to split ends, use your interests to find common ground. When you are younger it is near impossible to grasp that your parent is someone more than just "Mom" or "Dad," but as you start high school, you are presented with an incredible opportunity, as a maturing young adult, to develop a genuine relationship with those "old folks."

Keep a Journal

I know that you have probably heard this a million times in your life, but it is true that keeping a journal is one of the very best ways to record events, express yourself, and divulge secrets.

In particular, when you are a freshman and have yet to find a close friend and confidante, journals are perfect for talking about that cute guy in your biology class, moaning about your seemingly enormous homework load, and documenting the people, places, and things in your every day life. Even if you think that there is nothing interesting in your life to write about, jot some stuff down anyway. What may seem like the most mundane things now will become so much fun to read about years down the road when we are old, wrinkly, paying taxes, and maybe even having our own kids.

A journal can be a magnificent place to doodle and a great friend to confide in during this transformation from little kid to teenager. Everyone says that being in high school is supposed to be the best and most glorious time of our lives. Even if that's not always true, we're only high school freshmen once and it would be a shame to forget it.

Zest Books Teen Advisory Board, 2007–2008
From left: Carolyn Hou, Hannah Shr, Joe Pinsker, Maxfield J. Peterson

Become a Teen Advisor!

Zest Books is an exciting new line of smart and edgy books for teens. The members of the Zest Books Teen Advisory Board are an integral part of our company. They serve as interns and work on all aspects of the publishing process, from helping to develop new books to fact-checking and editing manuscripts. They also help keep things real in the office. Our teen advisors are from different high schools around San Francisco and were selected based on their interests and accomplishments in writing, reading, editing, and teen culture. If you are interested in becoming a teen advisor, send a letter of interest to us at *editorial@orangeavenue.com*.

To learn more about Zest Books, visit *www.zestbooks.net*.

JAN 1 4 2009